RULES OF 3

Focusing on your Flow

- Breaking Down The Journey of Triumph & Simplifying Success -

(A GUIDE TO HELP YOU PRIORITIZE & BUILD HEALTHY HABITS)

By
Simon Hawk

"To be honest, There are 3 options in life.

Fight, Flight or Sit. You choose."

- Simon Hawk -

INDEX

CHAPTER 1
DIRECTION & REACTION : 3 Choices in Life - Fight, Flight or Sit

CHAPTER 2
LIFESTYLE & LIFECHOICES : 3 Ways of Living - The Good, The Bad & The Ugly

CHAPTER 3
NUTRITION & NATURE : 3 Ways to Heal - Inside, Outside & In Business

CHAPTER 4
ACTION & EDUCATION : 3 Ways to Help - Yourself, Others & The Next Generation

CHAPTER 5
ORGANIC & PAID : 3 Ways to Grow - Plants, Partners & Parents

CHAPTER 6
RECYCLING & REPURPOSING : 3 Ways to Pivot - Left, Right or 180

CHAPTER 7
EBB & FLOW : 3 Ways to Profit - Streams, Rivers & Waterfalls

CHAPTER 8
SIZE & SPEED : 3 Ways to scale - Up, Down or Automate

CHAPTER 9
ONWARD & UPWARD : 3 Ways to succeed - Small, Big or XXXL

CHAPTER 10
SLOW & STEADY : 3 Ways to relax - Now, Later or Never

Afterthought - How to Sleep Better - Faster & Easier

CHAPTER 1

DIRECTION & REACTION : 3 Choices in Life - Fight, Flight or Sit

The way of the passive observer accomplishes little.
While this is fine for some who enjoy meditating.
Others will find the need to succeed.

The desire to "succeed" is often instilled in us at a young age.
Others develop it later in life after they receive an education.
Some will pick up a book like this & get inspired.

The primal instincts of Fight or Flight have adapted to a new way of life. There is rarely a NEED to fight anyone & most people seldom NEED to run anywhere. Most people are sitting more often than they are fighting or in flight.

This book was designed & written to force you to make a choice. You have 3 options in almost every scenario we will discuss in the chapters ahead. In each situation in life you will have the ability to Advance, Retreat or Wait.

Whether we talk about your business, your farm, your personal life or your romantic life, You will be provided with basic fundamental options on how to proceed. You can move forward, you can sit in the same space or you can go backwards.

Obviously there will always be many other options like pivoting or moving laterally. I did not write this book to go over endless semantics & hypothetical situations. I wrote these words, filled these pages & completed these chapters to simplify decisions.

As you may have noticed these paragraphs are created in a very specific way. Each statement will have 3 sentences throughout the book to keep it simple. This is my way of showing you at the very basic level how nice the rules of 3 can be.

In this book you will find options, not solutions.
In this book you will find opinions, not facts.
In this book, I hope you will find information.

This is not a boring business book or a way to format photos.
This is not a textbook full of facts or a regurgitation of data.
This is a book of poetry focused on guiding you.

CHAPTER 2

LIFESTYLE & LIFECHOICES : 3 ways of living - The good, the bad & the ugly

I have a favorite quote that I heard as a kid, it was in a movie that was dark & gritty. The scenes in Pulp Fiction were raw & showed me how difficult the world could be. This particular quote was used by a character who had to make difficult choices.

"The path of the righteous is beset on all sides by the iniquities of the selfish, & the tyranny of evil. Blessed is he who, in the name of charity & good will, shepherds the weak through the valley of the darkness. For he is truly his family's protector & the finder of lost children.'

In life we will be presented with many difficult choices, each one will allow us an opportunity. The quote above has become a mantra for me in extremely difficult times. Times when I have had to make a serious choice about what path I want my life to take.

At the beginning of my life I did not always make good decisions, some of them were bad. Up until my mid 20's a certainly made some ugly choices as well, i didn't know any better.
Oftentimes when we are uneducated or hurt or struggling, we make poor decisions.

The goal of this chapter is to show you that there are essential 3 choices of how you can live.
You can live your life in a good way, a bad way & an ugly way. It can be that simple. You are either doing a good thing, a bad thing or an ugly thing, you know it when you feel it.

Good things feel very good & often reward you with health, wealth & happiness. Bad things feel very bad & often end up in no result, poor results or bad results. Ugly things feel very & often result in a dangerous or deadly situation.

Obviously if you do nothing, very little happens normally & you get no results. Mediating is good, but doing absolutely nothing like watching TV endlessly is bad. There is the very likely scenario that doing nothing will lead to something bad, like eviction.

In regards to your style of life & the choices you make, you have 3 options. You can have a good, a bad or an ugly lifestyle develop from the corresponding choices. They say the suit makes the man, but the habits & choices are truly what makes a man.

I have taught myself many expensive lessons by making good, bad & ugly choices. I consider good choices, decisions made to help others in a healthy & happy way. I consider bad choices, decisions made to gain from others in an unhealthy & angry way.

Ugly choices are much more sinister & are made to hurt others in a destructive deadly way. In my opinion these decisions never need to be made, they are simply not necessary. Study any case of someone doing something ugly & you will see a sad story.

If you have made bad or ugly decisions in the past, this does NOT mean you can't change. Positive change is a good decision, which creates positive reactions & good outcomes. The best way to use the rule of 3 to make better decisions is as follows:

Devote ⅓ of your time to working on your career/business/education to get a paycheck.
Devote ⅓ of your time to personal growth/health/happiness/ to feel good about yourself.
Devote ⅓ of your time to social/romantic/family/community to connect with others.

The rule of 3 is very beneficial for helping you to focus on the three most important aspects. There are of course many other things in life to consider, especially if you have a complex life. When we focus on our core three, it simply allows us to maintain stability in our life.

Creating stability is the first step to becoming financially free, creating a home or a business. To become financially free we need stable income that we can rely on to pay for expenses.
To build a home we need a foundation poured & for business we need stable cash flow.

Stability will allow your partners in love & business to believe in your abilities as a leader. Without stability things are uncertain, which can lead to wives or employees to lose faith. When we lose faith we start to make bad decisions & in the end ugly things can happen.

This is especially true with romantic relationships & business, if you do not do good... Then you must be doing bad, which is just the ugly truth. There is not wrong with maintaining a stable business even if the income is low, that is good.

Any business is good business as long it is done in a healthy, happy & legal way. You do not necessarily need to strive to be a millionaire or even make $100k a year. It is a good goal to simply generate enough money to cover your expenses.

Later in this book we will talk about working 3 times harder & producing 3x results. For the sake of this chapter & those who are not over-achieving entrepreneurs, I want to be clear that there should not be unhealthy pressure to obtain more than needed.

A healthy balance developed by focusing on your core 3 should truly be the goal. If you are a farmer, a gardener, a teacher, a student, or a laborer, you can do as you please. You don't need to be in the top 3 of your league or compete with the big 4 in your industry.

No matter what profession, occupation or lifestyle you have chosen you still need balance. No one is able to only do one thing all of the time, so we are constantly balancing our time.
No time needs to be spent on bad or ugly decisions which should

make things easier.

Making a conscious decision to make good decisions is not always that easy. If you do it repeatedly you will find that it becomes a habit in 30 days. So all you need to do is make good decisions 3 days in a row & then repeat that ten times.

Performing tasks repeatedly builds skill incrementally, each repetition allows you to improve. By repeatedly making good decisions in your relationships, business & health you will grow. Years of continually doing good work , being good to your partner & body will heal you.

CHAPTER 3

NUTRITION & NATURE : 3 Ways to Heal - Inside, Outside & In Business

Considering that this book was written in 2020, the year of corona, I need to address health. While these pages are being typed many people are in fear, which is bad. What I hope to convey in this chapter are 3 ways to heal your mind, body & business.

Let us start with your mind as it controls both your body & your business. Your mind is your single most important tool, it must be protected & maintenance like a tool. You want to sharpen your mind, the same way we sharpen a machete to cut easier.

The sharper your mind is the better you will be able to solve problems in business. To begin healing your mind you need to provide it with proper nutrition & adequate nature. The chemical imbalances in the brain can often be solved through diet & exercise.

The key to healing your brain if you have done damage to it in the past is through nutrition. When we provide what the brain needs to function in abundance, it will heal itself. The proper combination of vitamins & minerals will allow your brain to rewire automatically.

The vitamins that people are normally missing in their diet for proper brain function include : PhosphatidylSerine, Huperzine A, Vitamin D3, omega-3 fatty acids, Ginkgo Biloba & Ginseng
These supplements are known to improve cognitive memory functions & improve memory.

*Please do your research when purchasing supplements as many products are misleading

** The article below explains that most brain boosting supplements are just caffeine pills -
*** Always educate yourself with real research - https://www.ncbi.nlm.nih.gov/pmc/articles/PMC7153641/

The basic nutrients needed for a healthy mind are often missed by most people, they include: Beta-carotene, Calcium, Fiber, Iron, Potassium, Magnesium, Vitamins B6, B12, C, D & E.
A regular diet of raw vegetables, fresh fruit, fresh fish & plenty of water will help.

I am not a nutritionist but I will tell you 3 things about myself that may help understand me. I have fluctuated from 150-160 lbs since I was 15, I am 35 now & have maintained my health.
I have traveled the world from Japan to the Caribbean & now invest in organic farming.

On my journeys across the planet I have learned much about food, culture & business. One thing all of them teach you is that diversity & variety are a very good thing. This is especially true if you are trying to heal. A diverse diet & exercise will help you.

Your organs function efficiently when they are properly fueled. I speak about this much more in depth in my second book "Fear or Food". If your mind or body is suffering, you must correct the imbalance before doing business.

Healing the brain is complicated because it is essentially a super-computer-muscle. The computer runs faster when you exercise & feed the muscle nutrients. To take action & actually retain the information you learn we must take care of our mind.

Exercising the mind can be done casually or in a very strenuous style that accelerates growth. Casual Mental Exercise - great for the elderly & children to develop or maintain memory. Strenuous Mental Exercise - best for students, researchers & workers developing skills

Casual Mental Exercises can be practiced regularly just like a training routine for sports. To keep the mind fit there are several great ways I will list 3 of them below.

1. Learn a new language or skill

2. Play puzzles or games

3. Make art or write creatively

There is an important concept called Neuroplasticity, which is important for brain function. In essence it is : The brain's ability to reorganize itself by forming new connections in life.
You can improve your brains organizing skills by practicing the tasks above.

Strenuous Mental Exercises can be practiced for extended periods of time to gain knowledge. Continually learning on a daily basis for large blocks of time by reading & listening is key.
You cannot hope to master any skill or improve in any area without dedicating time.

Once you dedicate large blocks of time repeatedly for weeks or months or even years,
You can develop an insight into any industry, any animal or any type of plant.
In horticulture we constantly study nature & how it can be used to heal or control the body.

If your mind is in the right place & functioning normally, you can easily control your body.
That takes us to the 3 ways that you can heal your body using your brain.
While placebo is a hell of a drug, I am talking about making smart choices for your body.

You can use your brain to research about your particular body weight & family history.
This will allow you to understand what you are working with &

working against.
You should always consult a medical physician & dietician before doing anything extreme.

This book in no ways advises you to take part in any fads, trends or unhealthy restrictive diets.
It is more important to provide your body with proper amounts of nutrition, this it.
If you are not at the weight or fitness level that is ideal for your body type, you can change.

Making a healthy change for your body does not mean getting obsessed with the gym.
It means you are prioritizing proper diet & exercise over poor diet & no exercise.
It is simply a choice to make your brain & body function better by purchasing better products.

The best products for your body are ones that are not filled with chemicals or contaminants. This means actively choosing fruits & vegetables from local farms that grow organically.
The other option is to grow food yourself, which we will discuss later in the book.

A wise & very healthy person to me is 1 of the best pieces of very simple advice for diet. He said "Eat the Rainbow"", which means to cook with natural ingredients of all colors. It suggests you should purchase a variety of fresh greens, fresh oranges & rainbow trout.

When we ingest fruits & plants our body is provided with macro & micro nutrients. When we ingest processed food or preservatives the beneficial nutrients are not present. We need to eat fresh, not frozen. Our bodies need nutrients, not chemicals.

This chemical culture has seeped into many other areas of life including business. It is quite common now for farms as a business to simply spray chemicals on plants. This is because it is easier to spray than change, but Making a change should be rewarded.

This way of doing things easier is bad & can turn ugly very quickly. Imagine a business that sold food that ends up poisoning its customers. How is this business model good for the people & why should we allow it to continue.

This style of commerce is seeping into many other industries, including manufacturing. When products are made now, they are designed to break sooner, so you buy more. This is called designed obsolescence & it good for profits, but very bad for people

Some companies think it easier to make a bad product that make alot of profit, Rather than making a good product that people do not need to buy repeatedly. Luckily there is a movement of people making things that last on purpose.

This is incredibly important as easy chemical culture has even soaked into marketing. Some advertisers find it easier to lie about their business or make false claims, Rather than making an honest claim & being transparent about their offer.

This can all be easily solved with a simple 3 step process to ensure what is done is good. Anytime you are designing a product, creating an offer or advertising a services ask this:

1. Will it help people?
2. Does the world need more of it?
3. Will this last 10-50 years?

If the answer is NO then you may want to consider NOT doing it. Do the world a favor. We do NOT need more one-time use products or disposable cups, ending up in landfills. What we need are real solutions, to real problems for real people. Not fake plastic replicas.

We need real leaders in business. We need to be realistic about how we can improve. If you realize your business model is flawed & do not know what to do, it's ok. You can always commit to making a change & take action to heal your business.

CHAPTER 4

ACTION & EDUCATION : 3 Ways to Help
- Yourself, Others & The Next Generation -

Taking action is incredibly important as nothing is done without putting in energy. Some people do not know where to put their energy & this is why education is key as well. When we take action to educate ourselves we can develop the ability to help others.

Have ever heard the phrase : "You cannot truly love others, until your learn to love yourself". The same goes for business : Ÿou cannot truly help others, until you have succeeded yourself". The same goes for education "You cannot truly teach others, until you have learned yourself"

If you really want to see action in your life, make a difference & educate others, You will need to do it first. You will need to take action & educate yourself differently. We must all love, help & teach ourselves first, so that we can do the same for others.

An entire community focused on positive actions, is not some fairytale fantasy concept. It exists currently in many forms. You will find them on the internet & in local businesses. There are whole groups dedicated to only sharing information that uplifts or educates.

If we continue to follow & give attention to mindless entertainment we cannot grow. To grow we need to take action daily & educate ourselves constantly on how to grow. You can grow even faster by dedicating time every day to learn about taking action.

There are 3 things that I want to focus on in regards to taking ac-

tion daily. **They are 1. Motivation 2. Rotation 3. Meditation**
Each aspect is incredibly important to maintaining consistent action.

Motivation - Each morning you will have a choice. You can choose motivation or distraction. Deciding to focus on motivating factors like health, wealth & happiness are a choice.
Motivating yourself can come in the form of exercise, diet, podcasts, videos, music & books.

Rotation - Each week you will have a rotation. You will start another cycle to improve upon. Switching up your routine & rotating through different diets helps with diversity. Rotating tasks keeps your motivation level high. Don't burn yourself out on a single activity.

Mediation - Each month you will have new data to consider. You can meditate on that. Analyzing the progress of your business & visualizing the path to success is meditation. Meditating is a very useful tool for motivating yourself. Sit quietly & think of your business.

If you use all three of these strategies you will see a drastic change in your energy for action. We must prepare for action, the same way we stretch before sports, we think before we act.
You cannot spend all of your time meditating or thinking about taking action though!

To help you manage your time & make a logical decision consider these 2 tips. 1. Dedicate 20% of your day to planning/thinking, 80% for taking action on plans/thoughts. 2. Take one day out of the week to plan/think about the rest of the week & write a schedule

When you have a schedule dedicated to taking action, you can break down a difficult task. Breaking down large jobs into daily tasks is the key to project management. Learning to take action, create schedules & manage timelines is important education.

When I went to highschool it seemed that the teachers were more interested in deadlines, Rather than teaching us how to manage timelines or create a schedule. For some reason that always seemed to be an assumed skill, when we see it needs taught.

This serious lack of training for real world skills & modern jobs has often left me confused. I sit & wonder even now about what could be done to properly prepare future students.
After many hours discussing education with business owners. This is what I have determined.

We need education on things that we repeatedly are faced with in life & business. We need to take action & begin requesting the information that is relevant to us. Considering that most businesses operate on similar principles I identified 3 areas of focus.

1. Financing different types of lifestyles, investing in businesses & managing credit/debt
2. Leading different types of people, speaking honestly/directly & managing employees
3. Sharing different types of information, opinions, research, invoices & digital currency

Imagine the world teenagers are entering into as you read this? Is it a world full of jobs? Do you think it is anything like what you experienced? Or is it a totally different job market?
Are the skills you learned in highschool still being used every single day? Probably not.

I love business math, but I still have not used algebra. This actually bothers me a lot. How much pressure could have been avoided if we focused on things we really need now. I could have skipped a lot of classes & just dedicated my time to learning what's relevant.

The answer to my problems & the systemic problem of poor

education is taking action. I have already educated myself on the things that I need to do repeatedly. The action I can take now is sharing that education & offering more information.

This book is my attempt to spur you into action & inspire you to educate yourself. You are strong. You are capable. You are intelligent. You are capable of great action. The moment you decide to take action & educate yourself, you will begin growing.

CHAPTER 5

ORGANIC & PAID : 3 Ways to Grow - Plants, Partners & Profits

In my opinion there are 3 main ways we grow into successful people later in life. Remember that no one starts out successful. Yes, some are given things later, But we are all born into nature naked & afraid. None of us are born rich.

Those who some might consider lucky are given riches at a very early age. If you study history though, it would seem that being GIVEN wealth is NOT always lucky. In many cases it completely ruins their experience on earth & fails to build character.

If I gave my kids candy all day or fed my plants only chemicals, they would be unhealthy. As parents we must provide proper nutrients to encourage optimal health & growth. As Partners in agriculture we need to agree to use natural methods & protect the soil.

When we protect the soil we can encourage long term growth which is sustainable growth. Massive growth when you are unprepared can be a very difficult thing to manage. Imagine if you planted a million seeds & then they all died because you only watered 100.

If you pay for a million advertisements but only have 100 products to sell what happens? You sell out of product quickly & then must advertise again once you restock. This is not a sustainable model & brings us to the point of this chapter.

When trying to determine how to grow we must consider the two options. You can either grow organically - putting in daily work & optimizing the process steadily. Or you can pay to grow - invest in speeding up the process & quickly adapting to growth.

In regards to Plants, it is simple to grow organically, never put chemicals on them. To grow organically simply provide the plant with compost, manure & water. Fresh organic soil with earthworms or mulch can be applied to the base of trees.

The paid alternative is to purchase organic plants from farms & plant them. To keep them organic, read the label before buying anything to feed your plant. If you cannot pronounce the name or when you google it, it is synthesized. Don't buy it.

In regards to Partners, it is slightly more complex as people can be difficult to deal with. Growing a partnership organically takes time, over years you develop a bond with someone. If a friend shows success, effort or capabilities, they could be a good potential partner.

The paid alternative is simpler as you can simply hire a partner, however this can be tricky. Ideally you want to be able to trust your partner deeply, so hiring someone randomly is hard.
A serious vetting process, a clear understanding of what you need & can afford is required.

In regards to Profits, it is fairly easy to organically grow profits. You simply sell one more unit. If every day you sell 1 more unit than the day before, you can organically grow your business.
Organic growth in profits is often attributed to word of mouth, reputation & location.

The paid alternative is fairly straightforward as you can simply pay for advertisements. If you run an ad that says what you offer, where to buy it, why it is good & how much it is…
People will buy your product! It's a numbers game. How many people can see your offer?

Those are the short & sweet answers. Obviously this whole book has been designed that way. It has been designed to give you 3 options & focus your mind on the top 3. I get bored when people start talking endlessly about possibilities & hypothetical situations

I wanted to give you the first 3 things that come to mind, the most important 3 factors. I tried to provide you with my perspective, the truth & the facts, not a bunch of theory. I am not here to teach you a lesson or prove you wrong, simply to offer you insight.

Insight is something you need to develop good partnerships, grow plants & profits. You must inform yourself about the people you aim to work with if you are to be successful.
Without insight you won't know what is wrong with your plants or if you are losing profits.

The one universally good thing about growing slowly & organically, is you have time. You have time to adapt, you have time to adjust & you have time to allow yourself a break. When you grow organically you are not putting stress on any system or overloading anyone.

The reality of growing quickly by paying for speed is the opposite, it is constantly a race. You will be forced to adapt, may need to pivot abruptly & you will have less breaks. As you run ads you must prepare for more sales, too many sales & you need more products.

Supply & demand often play a large factor in whether to grow organically or pay for speed. If your business runs out of supplies & there is a large demand for the product, buy more fast!
If there is a rush, you may pay a premium, but still profit. If there's no rush, order in bulk.

If the demand for a product is low, running ads for it may not help as no one wants the offer. Growing a brand organically & creating demand by raising the perceived value is smart.
Creating a following organically by sharing free content is the op-

posite of the paid model.

There's much debate over which is better online, however there is no need for competition. Both can be used equally or to varying degrees. This is another great place for the 80/20 rule.
I personally suggest that in most cases 80% of your growth should be organic & 20% paid.

If you have just started farm & wanted to grow it quickly by selling fruit from 100 trees, You may want to consider buying 20 mature trees that are fruiting & plant 80 more.
This strategy would ensure that you could sell fruit & have future more profitable harvests.

Buying all mature trees would cost more than you would profit putting you in debt. Planting all the trees from seed would allow for slow growth leaving you with no profit. The hybrid of both strategies is the sweet spot, the overlapping point of mutual benefit.

If you are just starting a business & wanted to grow it quickly by selling 100 products, You can consider spending 80% of your budget on organic sales calls & 20% on ads. In the beginning of a business it is important to grow your brand & expand as you are able.

A business with a small budget, no sales team, low demand & low supply is fragile. There is not a lot of room for error or large profit margins to allow for unnecessary spending. The hybrid strategy is best for small businesses as it allows them to test ads & then invest.

If you are seeking to grow your profits & want to do it quickly by selling 10x more products, You may consider spending 80% of your marketing on organic campaigns & 20% on ads.
The hybrid approach is just a good rule of thumb for segmenting your time or resources.

If you are serious about growing your business & investing in making more profit, It is not a good idea to put all of your eggs in one basket. Old saying, but still true. Diversifying your investment strategies is an excellent way to mitigate risk & loss.

No matter which road you take, you will be met with challenges, much like a triathlon. Letting these hurdles or roadblocks stop you, is not a good strategy for growth. Preparing for things to change, by expecting shifts is smart & allows you to pivot.

CHAPTER 6

RECYCLING & REPURPOSING : 3 Ways to Pivot - Spin, Slide & Lean

The world's changing & there are many people that need to pivot right now, you may be one.
Pivoting in business is when what's working no longer works & you change your strategy.
No matter what happens in the world, business must continue, so you have to make it work.

One thing most serious business owners agree on is that you don't give up when it gets hard.
When sales get slow, business accounts are drained & motivation is at an all time low,
It is a good time to make a pivot. You can do this by spinning, sliding & leaning.

It may sound like a funny dance & you can certainly do a dance once you have succeeded.
Pivoting is a serious solution to serious problems that arise, like a global health pandemic.
If you can succeed in a recession, a quarantine or a natural disaster, then you can celebrate

I personally see 2 clear directions to pivot towards if you are at a complete loss for what to do.
In hard times it is incredibly important to be resourceful & resilient if you hope to succeed.
The easiest ways to create a profit when you have nothing is to recycle & repurpose.

I am not talking about digging through the trash, however if you

find this book in the trash,
With no other options other than read it, I encourage you to sell this book or paint all over it.
If you sell it, you have essentially recycled it or if you make it into art, you have repurposed it.

This same mentality can be used for small businesses & giant corporations as well.
If you happen to be a CEO & ordered this book online, you can still recycle & repurpose.
Think about all the content your company has made over the lifetime of your business...

Just because your marketing budget disappears does not mean you cannot recycle content.
If you pay homage to your roots, pay tribute to your past or celebrate your journey, it works.
An amazing way to make something from nothing is to repurpose old content into new ads.

There are 3 main points that I want to make in regards to pivoting in a positive way.
It is important to note there are many other directions to take & pivoting can be negative.
When something is working continuously & customers are happy there's no need to pivot.

The 3 most important things to review before making a hasty decision to pivot are as follows.
1. Why are we pivoting 2. When are we going to pivot 3 How are we going to pivot
Before deciding to change a product we must review the CAUSE & EFFECT of each..

WHY? It is very common for businesses to pivot out of fear. Fear of losing profits or products.
CAUSE - Carefully analyze how the fear was created & what the root of the problem is

EFFECT - Consider what will happen if you act on fear & respond to the problem by pivoting

WHEN? It frequently happens that businesses see they need to pivot & then don't commit
CAUSE - Determine exactly what is holding you back from pivoting & address it directly
EFFECT - Understand the consequences of not taking action & allowing others to succeed

HOW? It is very rare for anyone to determine the best course of action, ask questions!
CAUSE - If a pivot is necessary because of unhappy clients ask them what they need changed
EFFECT - Think about what will happen to your sales if your customers get what they need

They say For every action there is an equal reaction & so there is always a cause & effect.
When clients are unhappy, sales are low. When you improve customer service, sales improve.
If an item looks bad, it won't sell. If you improve the packaging & marketing, sales improve.

Once you have considered the reasoning & implications for making a pivot, it's time to act.
With so many potential directions to move towards, it is important to make a pivot plan.
It's just like drawing a map from Point A - Point B. Where you are vs where you want to go to.

A pivot plan can be extremely simple if you are a LLC or a complex document for a S-Corp.
It all depends on who you are talking to & consider the desperate nature of most pivots,
I would not waste any time writing elaborately if you need to get straight to the point.

The ideal minimal pivot plan would be extremely blunt, very direct, void of any fluff or fear.
The idea is to communicate exactly what is going on, what will be done & when.
This ideally ties back to the 3 things you considered before deciding to pivot.

1. PIVOT WHY - Customers have complained that product A is bad, now sales are low.
2. PIVOT WHEN - Stop selling product A on X date & send refund with an offer for Product B.
3. PIVOT HOW - Pull all content relating to product A & replace with Product B.

This obviously over simplifies some very complex issues, but at its core this works.
Solving problems should not cause more problems. There are simple solutions to all things.
Even the most complex of machines all have one similar function. ON or OFF.

This minimalist problem solving mentality needs to be explored the more complex life gets.
Complex thought must occur for us to create successful solutions & intelligent decisions.
No matter how you came to the conclusion, the execution will be easier if it is simpler.

We do not strive to reduce the quality of a solution, only analyze at what expense it comes at.
A simple solution is often cheap, effective, efficient & sustainable to repeat if needed.
A complex solution usually involves multiple people, is slow to execute & often expensive.

In my experience the most complex solutions are created by lawyers, politicians & marketers.

Complicated programs & strategies to solve problems are just a waste of time, money or both.
There are many extreme examples of these three groups perpetually selling information.

I know this first hand, because I have worked with lawyers & listened to politicians.
I know exactly what marketers do, because I have worked as one & studied their strategies.
I am now a management consultant, so I know exactly how the billable hours game works.

It's like this: If they could solve your problem quickly, That would be good for you, not them.
If they had 10 hungry kids in front of them, they would pay their friends to make a plan to feed them using money they got from someone else, instead of just feeding the kids.

That is just the world we live in. That does not mean you have to perpetuate the stereotype.
If you are or are aspiring to be a lawyer, a politician or a marketer, then do it. Just do it right.
We need intelligent people who know why they are pivoting, when to pivot & how to pivot.

If you find you are in the right profession, but on the wrong path, now is the time to pivot.
Maybe your partners or colleagues made some bad decisions & now it's time to roll out.
There are a few ways to pivot with style & I will go over them with you now.

SPIN - a spin move is when shift & then circle back to head in the same direction.
This move can be used to leave a position or niche & continue on after considering options.
When you spin around you look in all directions before coming back to center.

This allows you to observe what is going on in the industry & then redefine your direction.
By pivoting quickly you can assess what is working for your competitors & adapt.
Keep in mind that you can spin out of control constantly looking at what others are doing.

If you start to lose your direction & find yourself spinning out of control, try to focus.
Do not get Analysis Paralysis by constantly scrolling, looking at your competition.
Remember to come back to the reason why you wanted to change & your plan.

SLIDE - A slide is much smoother than a spin & often is the best choice if things get bad.
A simple slide can be focusing on a product that is doing well & stop selling a bad product.
Sliding takes the least effort, as you are really just doing the minimum required to succeed.

A sliding pivot is a good way to make a subtle change or casually redirect your efforts. Not every business requires dramatic change during an economic depression. Some industries do relatively well when things are bad & only need small changes to profit.

A great example of an incredible underground slide maneuver was performed by Elon Musk. When he realized that LA & many cities had a serious traffic problem for his vehicles,
He simply pivoted slightly & started making underground tunnels. No big deal.

Another revenue stream for the Tesla founder, but for others it could be a genius solution. To a man like Elon Musk the solution to the problem & meetings about it were boring, so he named the company The Boring Company, it's funny because they bore holes.

Get it?

A slide can be done in a career if you are unsatisfied with the work you are currently doing. I have personally helped many people slide from being an employee to a consultant. In many cases there was no actual change in their routine, just a slide to a new title.

Sliding from one type of business model, but staying in the same industry is totally possible. I highly advise you to always be considering better strategies for servicing your market.
If your client needs a solution no one else offers, there may be profit to be made from it.

This type of slide is happening all over the globe for farmers as they shift to growing hemp. The cultivation of high CBD flowers & industrial hemp has given farms a new opportunity.
Pivoting your business to produce/sell a highly profitable product is always a smart decision.

LEAN - My favorite of the 3 pivoting styles I focus on is not evasive, it is aggressive. Leaning in is a term used for applying more force & pushing forward positively. I love to lean into a problem & push for a solution, even when it ruffles some feathers.

If you're getting good results or are completely confident in your direction, it's time to lean in! When you start smelling the fear in your competition & they start to back down, lean in more! If you start to see success, where others have failed or while they are failing, lean in harder!

You do not need to solve everyone's problem, during a crisis you need to take care of yourself. You need to take care of your staff, clients, family, friends, & community. That is it. You can't save the world, so don't try. Start by saving those directly around you. Start local.

Locally is an excellent place to lean in, especially if sales are low, but your reputation is good. If you are known in your community for taking care of your clients, make them more offers. Start leaning into local ads, communicate with local business owners & offer services.

International markets are always a good place to lean into if your local market slows down. I speak with farmers about this quite often in fact as shipping things like coffee bring higher
Profits from international customers than it does from locals. Simple supply & demand.

If what you have is very common in your area, but is off very high quality, you can lean in! High quality packaging paired with a great product can create serious profits, if sent to
The right location where that item is very rare & highly sought after by wealthy people.

This is exactly why the french & the italians export wine to the rest of the world.
In Italy a great bottle of wine is so common that paying extra for normal is absurd to locals.
Ship the same "normal" bottles to New York & you instantly have a superior & rare item.

Deciding not to pivot & lean in because of fear is foolish, I compare it to pouring out a great bottle of wine without tasting it because the bottle has a sticker that says might not be good.
I did not grow up in a house where we had money to throw out wine, we used it for cooking.

The idea of having money to pour out wine didn't occur to me as a possibility till my teens.
When I started noticing what other families had I started to ask questions more.
Many of my questions didn't get answered, so I pivoted & went looking for answers.

What I found when I went looking was incredible, I found endless options & examples.
Hundreds of ways to recycle, thousands of ways to repurpose &

millions of ways to profit.

When I moved to the Island of Puerto Rico in 2015 I truly started to see a new direction.

I met very wealthy people who worked hard their whole lives, all had pivoted at one time.

Each successful person I met, I try to ask them how they came to gain success & profits.

Each & every one of them had a story about pivoting to new revenue streams.

CHAPTER 7

EBB & FLOW : 3 Ways to Profit - Streams, Rivers & Waterfalls

I came to a realization early on that everything in life comes in the form of waves. Waves of light, sound waves, ocean waves, emotional waves, even DNA looks like a wave. This up & down cycle is basically an ebb & flow of energy.

If you imagine the flow of energy in a business as money, you'll see why it is called cash flow. The cash flow of a business is the lifeblood that supports the staff & their families. Without cash flow a business can die & families cut off from their lifeline.

It is important as an employer or a business owner to be considerate of how you hire. If you cannot support a new staff member, you should not hire them. Projecting revenue & hiring based on inaccurate information can lead to financial ruin.

I have seen firsthand with my cannabis consulting clients the errors of neglected cash flow. It is easy as a startup business to perpetually spend money without making any. This habit of raising money, just to spend money is unsustainable.

In this chapter I outline 3 ways to make money in a sustainable way. It is wise to start a sustainable business as it reduces your stress & allows for organic growth. I have watched as many bosses, managers & investors lose their shit over unachieved goals.

It is better to be realistic about how much you can make & project accurate financial data. When you make a projection you can set a goal for a High Quota & a Low Quota. By setting a sliding scale you can accurately represent what may happen.

A low quota for sales is simply the worst possible scenario. Your worst month last year is your Lowest quota, because this is based on real data. You can expect the same this year.
Ideally you would do better than last year, so this would be where you set a high quota.

I think it is very achievable to grow by 3X on a regular basis, some say 10, but let's be real. You can certainly work twice as hard as you are now & I bet you can work 3 times harder.
I don't believe if you are working a 6 hour shift that you can work 60 hours a day. Maybe 18.

If you had 18 hours in a day to get work done, imagine how productive you would be. Some people are already at this level, if you are really serious about success, you would be too.
Whenever you are ready to take life head on, decide to wake up at 3AM & go to bed at 9PM.

If you only do it for 3 days out of the week I guarantee you will see better results & revenue. Sometimes this is just what it takes, if you are interested in an intense period of growth,
I challenge you to join me in an online course called "The Catalyst Program" SIGN UP NOW!

In The Catalyst Program I walk my students through a system that teaches them to profit. It is a breakdown of how to launch a business or product quickly & explains how to profit.
If you are interested in getting 99 days of training to become better at business JOIN ME

The three ways that I teach people to profit are all about different types of flow rates. Since cash flow comes at different speeds it is important to establish which is which first.
You obviously want as much cash flow as possible, so it's common to use all 3 types at once.

Large businesses that make a lot of profit fast have a high cash flow. I call them Waterfalls. Medium size businesses making average profit have a medium cash flow. I call them Rivers.
Small businesses that make a low profit slowly, have a low cash flow. I call them Streams.

Nature is the ultimate example of flow, small streams carry water slowly, big rivers flow quickly & waterfalls are a tremendous surge of power & energy as water rushes down.
If your business's cash flow was one of these, you would want it to be a waterfall.

Waterfalls are very powerful images, it is a constant power fueled by gravity. As long as the flow of water continues this channel will create constant energy. If a big business can constantly fund it's marketing & sales team, profits will continue.

Interestingly, even a very small business can have a revenue stream that is a waterfall. Take for example an ecommerce site that has 3 employees but sells $3M in CBD products. This very small company could continue to fund its marketing & sales team easily.

Planning for the building of a waterfall is slightly harder than just finding a natural one. This is the difference between Organic & Paid marketing for high volume revenue streams. You can create demand through paid ads or address a current need with organic content.

While they say that you should not go chasing waterfalls, I disagree in this context. You should constantly be on the hunt for where you can position yourself to profit. The goal is to find a niche or customer who demands what you have & the supply is low.

Too many people profiting from one revenue stream can suck a waterfall dry. A waterfall can easily turn into a river, a stream, a trickle or a straight up dam. When the cash flow stops the waterfall of money ceases. No water, No life.

So it is important to realize when an industry or a niche has lost it's flow. It is also highly possible that you have lost your flow, or your mojo. If this happens to you, I want you to stop, drop, shut down those feelings & open up shop.

Open up shop under a new waterfall & let the money rain down again. You can always move. People forget this, but it is very natural for animals & people to migrate. When things stop working you can pick up & go to a different town, industry or website.

If you run out of waterfalls & everything seems dried up it is ok. Things change! You can always create many different smaller channels of revenue that equal the same flow. Micro-transactions are an example of this. 1,000,000 sales at $1 profit, is still $1 Million in profit.

Rivers have plenty of flow with some rapids & can certainly sustain life. A cash flow that is a river can easily support a staff & allow you to invest in increasing flow. Many rivers of profit can be developed to create the same cashflow as a waterfall.

A perfect example of a river you can set up is a food based delivery business. If you have a farm & can sell your customers food. It may not make you rich, But it will be a steady flow of profit that will allow you to hire a farmhand & delivery staff.

If you had a dozen farms, you could easily generate millions of dollars in profit a month. This is the power of investing in agriculture & people. People grow food. Not the internet. River revenue can be rural, it doesn't have to involve tech at all. Even a simple restaurant franchise can generate millions in revenue.

If you study business or film you may have come across the story of Ray Crock. Ray was the man behind franchising the McDonald's brand out & making it famous. Before it was famous it was an unknown hamburger shop with a good automation system.

These lessons that can be learned from other mistakes or misfortunes often can help us. There are many ways to avoid problems & take a higher road that is more ethical. When you learn from the past, it can be much easier to get into a successful flow.

Ray realized that this river of revenue could be multiplied & turn it into a waterfall. The original founders of the concept Dick & Mac Mcdonald, did not agree & rejected him. He went on to do the idea for anyone & use most of their ideas, he paid for some rights.

What the original founders failed to realize was he was right. There was more profit to be had. They were missing out on duplicating, expanding & monetizing their business model.
They failed to see that he was chasing waterfalls, in the end they got left with a stream.

STREAMS are small channels of water that flow slowly with little power & support little life.
It is very rare to power a whole company on a single stream of revenue with low cash flow. A side hustle is a nice stream of income at a low rate with a low amount of resources needed.

A single stream of income for an individual is fine. If you have a solid job & you like it simply, by all means continue forward on your path, but only if it is completely fulfilling to you.
If there is a need in your life that is not possible with a single stream of revenue, add another!

You could literally have hundreds of different streams of revenue. Most can handle 3-5 easily. To give you an example, for years my partner & I have done the following.
1. Renovat Homes 2. Work on farms 3. Consult clients online

These 5 streams of revenue allowed us to travel the world together & live comfortably. It was incredible to be able to walk away from a stream knowing another would support us. No matter where we went on the planet, we knew one of our services would be in demand.

This for us was a huge revelation. We had an epiphany as a couple & found our flow. We took all of our revenue streams & increased the cashflow turning them into rivers. Then we hired people to manage the rivers & started hunting for waterfalls.

The lakes, rivers & streams that we were used to were simply not enough anymore. This happened for three reasons in my opinion, based on my observation most people face the same problems we did.

1. We saw that others had multiple streams of income

2. We audited our companies expenses vs profits and detemined we needed more cash flow.

3. We realized we needed more capital to build make a bigger impact

Ultimately we needed to increase the size or our company & increase the speed of cash flow.
We realized this because we had bigger ambitions. If you are content where you are at, it's ok. This book was written for people who won't grow bigger & get faster.

CHAPTER 8

SIZE & SPEED : 3 Ways to scale - Space, Staff & Sales

When we talk about the scale of things, we talk about how big they are or how fast they are. "The building was incredibly designed & 10 Million square feet, it was massively impressive."
"The car was amazingly constructed & went a 0-100 in 4.2 seconds, it was incredibly fast."

An perfect example of a company that has scaled to incredible sizes at record speed, is Tesla. The electric car company, at the time this book was written, has skyrocketed literally. Recently the company's founder repeatedly launched into space his new company's rockets.

The founder of Paypal turned sustainable energy giant, can teach us much about scaling. His companies continue to innovate in every sector from management to battery efficiency.
This is all made possible by designing great systems, hiring great leaders & staying focused on creating solutions.

These 3 key components of scaling a company are at the very core of business as well. When you develop a great system for doing business you can then automate it. When you hire great leaders they can ensure the systems & automation are maintained. When you focus on creating solutions you can pivot easily & profit from more situations.

There will always be a human element to automation & technology.
Many intelligent leaders including Elon Musk have commented

on the use of AI in business.
It is a tricky thing to try to anticipate the future or predict what will happen, but we can try.

My theory is this: Anything that is done repeatedly without thought should be automated.
I predict that: Robotics & intelligent software will make life better for labor in manufacturing.
I anticipate: Machine Learning & AI will reduce the risks associated with human errors

These in my opinion are all very good things. There will always be a need for people to design.
Sure robots can design things, but what makes humans special is their ability to create.
Machines are made by us to help us create more things, easier & faster.

I think that humans need to embrace machines & find a way to reduce their need for fuel.
Electric/solar/battery powered machines certainly seem to be the way to go in the future.
Reducing our dependence on fossil fuels is intelligent, we can use renewable resources now.

When it comes to scaling your own company, it may not involve Robots or AI at all. That's fine.
What most people fail to realize is that they can still use Automation & Software to help.
If you are interested in increasing the size or speed of your company, consider automating.

Automation is best done with software, however on the farm it is often done by a machine. Packaging & harvesting equipment are great examples of lowtech robots that help us.
Without these human-designed hunks of metal cut into gears,

we'd need 100's of laborers.

In every day business we use laser printers, coffee machines, drones & phones regularly now. Each one of these items is an automated machine & a low-tech robot with some AI in it.
We are lucky to be born in a generation where these tools are available to benefit us.

Automation is good. You do not want to waste your time manually entering data. Scaling a company is good. You do not want to do everything yourself & lose clients. Speeding up cash flow is good. You do not want to stop yourself from being successful.

There are 3 ways you go when you are scaling your company. All of them can increase speed.

1. You can Scale Up

2. You can Scale Down

or

3. You can Automate yourself out

Each option comes with a different set of responsibilities & unique advantages.

All 3 of them can be done in unison to create a truly lean & sustainable business model. I highly suggest doing them all in some form or another. Constantly cutting the fat is good. You want to be a lean hungry proud profitable lion. Not a lazy fat boring bored lion.

No offense if you read this & have a weight issue. I think you should deal with that first. Before doing business we need to be healthy. I am not saying you can't do big business, If you are a big person. But let's be honest, you won't live as long & do as much business.

If you were truly dedicated to scaling your company & increasing speed, you would change. Making changes is good. Trimming fat is good. Exercise is good. Improving your body is good. Don't take on more projects to avoid taking care of your health. Before you scale, get fit first.

SCALING UP - To scale up you are going to need three things 1. Space 2. Staff 3. Sales Most businesses need to be able to scale to take on more bigger clients or projects. This means they need more resources to allow them to grow & become more profitable.

SPACE - This can be in regards to the size of the market, office size or farmland to expand. In the market you must be sure there is more profit to be had & you area can support growth.
Your office must be able to handle expansion & your farm has room to make new fields.

If these aspects are lacking you will need to plan for a shift when you scale up. Get ready! To scale your company you may need a better location, second location or bigger place. To scale your company you may need to get access to more land or clear space for planting.

You will need to make space to scale into the market if there is none. Diversifying is good. When a company diversifies it can make room for scaling. Taking on a new market is smart.
If you want to scale your company you may need to find new products or services to sell.

STAFF - This is straight forward, as more clients or projects you take the more staff you need. Hiring great staff is dependent on a well designed hiring & training program. It is essential that multiple candidates are interviewed & recruited systematically onboarded.

Scaling up does not always mean paying 100 salaries & filling a building with people. You can easily outsource much of the work you need done & use automation. I will speak about this later in the section regarding Scaling down.

I have personally identified 3 essential staff members that a business needs to scale.

1. **Personal/Virtual Assistant**
2. **Sales Executive**
3. **Operations Manager**

These 3 people can allow a break-even one-man-show to turn into a profitable machine.

You may not even realize it right now, but you may be doing all these roles yourself right now. Or even worse, you are asking/demanding your wife or partner or children or friends to do it.
The problem with that is, that's not their job. You need to find the best person for the job.

That is really the key to scaling & staff. FIND THE RIGHT PERSON, FOR THE RIGHT JOB. Do not ask a graphic designer to do coding. Do not ask a management consultant to clean.
It is inappropriate & foolish to think that you can just request people to get good at things.

People are motivated by different things & skilled in different areas. Do not try to put a big round peg in a tiny square hole. It will not work. You need to find someone who is good at the job & wants to do the job.

The best staff members motivate themselves, because they truly want to do a good job. Not because you tell them they have to or threaten to fire them. That is bad management.
Instilling responsibility, respect & encouraging growth is done through great leadership.

When you pick your top 3 candidates for your 3 core positions, think about this:

"Who do you want to work with & speak to on a daily basis?"
"How will hiring the right person affect me vs. hiring the wrong person?"

When you pick your staff, think of them as team members, you are gathering an all star team. There needs to be something that unites the team, whether it is money or passion. Own it.
Tell them why & how you want things done in the beginning so they know what to expect.

You are building a team of people to support your business, make sure to appreciate that. They are there to help you, because you asked them to join you. This is a big responsibility.
You have become a team leader, a manager, a role model, a boss & a lion

SALES - The key to scaling a company is making more sales. Lions hunt, Businesses Sell.
You are either selling a product, a service or an opportunity. To scale you need to sell more.
This is why it is so important to have more staff & more room for them to work.

It is hard to make more sales, if you have no one making more sales calls.
Your company can easily increase revenue by 300% simply by making 3X more sales calls.
If you only call one client this month how many sales do you think you could hope for?

One. A sale is the most you can make from a sales call. Now if that 1 call profits $1 million,
You are good. However, Most sales calls generate anywhere from $100-$3,000 on average.
So if you have a product that profits $3k, you need to make 333

calls to make $1 million.

Of course you can call someone & sell them multiple products, this would be smart to do!
Of course you can include multiple people in one call & make hundreds of sales, do that now!
Of course you can record a sales call & turn it into & ad & sell millions, definitely do that!

Ultimately you will need to repeat this process to scale. You will need to call, record & include,
MORE PEOPLE! This is the key to scaling, you need more people to buy from you more often.
This of course is done by investing in sales & a sales staff. A sales executive is the first step.

To make more sales I highly suggest improving your sales system. Here are 3 ways to do that:

1. Chart the Customer Journey
2. Write a Sales Script
3. Use a CRM System

These 3 strategies can very quickly allow you to scale your company & help your staff adapt

Charting the Customer Journey - can be done by simply illustrating the steps your customer must take to go from cold call or first contact to purchasing a product from you. This is an excellent exercise as you may find it requires many many steps to make a sale.

If you find that your process for making a sales requires more than 10 steps, it may be time to redesign your system or address the problem. Some businesses this is just how it is. To get the contract to build a building is harder than selling a box full of roses or chocolate.

Whatever your business is you need to understand what is required to make a sale. If you can simplify this process to 3 simple steps or 3 phases, you will get more sales faster. The easier it is for people to buy from you, the more often they will buy.

When I talk about making more sales, I do not recommend doing anything shady. There are many ways to make more sales ethically & it is not complicated, so don't be shady.
Here are several examples of very simple 3 step sales systems that are used globally.

1. Call potential clients from list of leads 2. Read Sales Script. 3. Ask for Sales on phone
This is a very old style of selling called cold-calling & has worked for many years. People like to speak directly about large purchases & major life impacting decisions.

1. Run ad for product online

2. Direct Potential client to Website

3. Ask for sales in copy.

This is an expensive, but effective way to get more sales. It is the oldest trick in the book. You can run ads online easily now on Facebook, Instagram, Google, Youtube & Pinterest.

1. Send email to customer list

2. Follow up with potential clients.

3. Ask for Sale via e-mail.

This a very inexpensive method that is fairly effective, many people don't open salesly e-mails. A salesly email can be redesigned to be conversational, informative, friendly or helpful. Creating automated email sequences is something that is fairly new & should be discussed.

This process is incredibly important for website sales & ecommerce businesses. Automated Email Sequences are awesome & can be designed to flow like a conversation. Whenever a customer purchases or adds a product to a shopping cart, But don't buy it.

An email sequence can be used to send the potential client a sequence of Emails conveying the value & overcoming objectives preventing them from purchasing. Making things easier to purchase is really at the heart of getting more business & sales.

If you provide a valuable solution, that is easy to understand & easy to purchase. You win! If you don't have that or a system to do this, design one right now, or ask for help! Scaling a company can potentially be difficult on existing staff members or become stressful.

This is often because the systems were not set up properly & now you have more problems. Avoid this by designing the systems needed to handle the staff before scaling. The size of the company matters greatly & usually small companies make a small profit.

It is not impossible for a very sustainable & productive group to be highly profitable. When a company grows larger organically the staff can handle growth & profits increase.

CHAPTER 9

ONWARD & UPWARD : 3 Ways to succeed
- Small, Big or XXXL

Growth only has two main directions, onward & upward, as you cannot grow backwards. We all hope profits will continue to grow upwards, but in fact sometimes they go down. Success is the continual growth of profits despite the occurrence of losses.

There are 3 main ways to succeed, in a small way, in a big wall or an XXXL way. This is completely dependent on your desires, goals & amount of dedication put in. For every action there is an opposite & equal reaction that occurs, even in success.

If your desires are small you may have ended up with a small amount of success. If you have medium sized goals you should expect to achieve a medium amount of success. If you put an extra large amount of dedication in, you will likely get a higher rate of success.

Success is a funny thing, it can seem elusive at times & hard to reach, until you have it. Once most people get a small amount of success they desire a little more success. This is achievable if you believe in yourself & are surround with people that believe in you.

A small amount of success does not require a large operation or a large team. In fact most small businesses are operated by 1-3 people. In many cases there is 1 employee.

Due to the fact that your operation is small it is hard to expect greater success. A small amount of success can be satisfactory. This book doesn't demand extreme measures. In many small businesses that goal of the operation is to exist on a small amount of profit.

There are many cases where business owners design smaller operations to reduce stress. A simple way to have success in medium size goals is to have small successes in several areas.
One can hope to do well by diversifying or multiplying their locations or investments sales.

Several cafes, multiple farms or a dozen shops will take a small success to a medium success. A medium amount of success is more easily obtained with a medium sized team. Offices with sales teams, software developers & medium size farms require teams of 10-20.

The more employees or hands working the faster medium sized projects are completed. A medium amount of effort is required to obtain a medium amount of success. It is perfectly acceptable to not want a large house or large farm, medium is manageable.

There are a few cases of people achieving great success with medium effort but it is rare. The simplest way to have an extreme amount of success & achieve extra extra extra large goals is to put in a very very very large amount of effort. This means you are committed 300%! The excessive amount of force required to overcome the inevitable obstacles results in stress.

XXXLarge amounts of success come at a toll, this payment or requirement is deep dedication. 100's of hours a week are absolutely necessary to gain XXXLarge levels of success. A very large team will be required to take on a goal of gigantic proportion.

A great example of an XXXL goal is a resort in a large building with many large rooms. This type of operation will take 100's of people to construct & operate. This is no easy task. The success that can be achieved from a resort is very high, thus the stress is equally high.

As you take on larger & larger goals, you will find that there builds a power in you. This power & confidence will be partnered with equally stressful or depressing feelings. This is natural as great rewards come at great risks. The larger you are the harder you fall.

There is not enough said of the pitfalls of pursuing XXXL goals. They are to be avoided. The pursuit of XXXL goals can be consuming & detrimental to health if not done right. The right way to pursue XXXL goals is to surround yourself with a very intelligent staff.

The thing about working with intelligent staff is that they are easy to offend & upset. When working with smart people, you must treat them with respect, in order to get respect. Far too often in my life I've met people with XXXL goals & an inability to be respectful.

A disrespectful attitude towards staff, clients or strangers is the wrong way to get any success. The current culture has proven that celebrities, CEOs & charities can be ruined by bad press.
In the future if you hope to have XXXL amounts of success you will have to be kind.

Being kind does not mean you let people walk all over you. That is the path to failure.
Kindness can be used while remaining very firm about your expectations or experience.
Using kindness as a strategy to gain an XXXL amount of success is always positive.

On a large scale it has been shown that when a corporation adopts a policy of kindness,
The consumer's perception of the brand changes & organic referrals increase.
When a company does not need to advertise due to their reputation, they will be successful.

Each way to reach success requires a different amount of time. It is easy to get impatient.
The larger your goals the longer they will take to achieve in most cases. Remember to relax.
The long term goal can be quite larger while your short term goals are smaller. Plan for both.

My personal advice to you is to have a mix of all. I personally have very small goals daily.

My monthly & yearly goals however are much larger. Large goals are my favorite.
XXXLarge goals are cool, but I personally am not interested in a XXL staff or XXL stress.

That is a choice you need to make. Do not expect to have large goals & no stress.
That is not the way it works. If you want a life with no stress, you must plan it that way.
It is possible to have such a good staff & team, that even XXXLarge goals become easy.

When you are ready to begin having more success you simply need to make a plan. If you are looking for a simple solution to your problems I offer you this quick tip : Do 3x more.
You can always call 3x more customers, send 3x as many emails or text 3x more clients.

You can continually improve your businesses revenue 3x by increasing your sales staff by 3. If your product is good & you need more sales you may want to buy 3x more leads to call.
When you are ready to sell 3X as many products, you may want to invest in 3x the ad budget.

Your amount of effort & investment in growth will be the biggest factor behind your success. You cannot hope to achieve medium or large or XXXL goals without investing in your growth. Your growth does not need to be extreme, or fast or stressful, just remember this.

You are not in a race. You may have competitors in your industry, but you will be your biggest competition that you will face. You are the single biggest threat to your own success. The speed at which you achieve success should be relative to your needs as a company.

Achieving many things at great speeds can be a recipe for disaster if not done correctly. Great speeds require great planning & support. You can easily anticipate disasters. Disasters will occur, this is part of Murphy's Law. "Anything that can go wrong will go wrong."

Murphy's law reminds us that whatever potential failures are possible, will indeed occur. Over time, especially when we operate or grow at great speeds, there are faster failures. When we grow a company quickly, there are more opportunities for failures & burnout.

Burning out on the job is a result of poor planning & extreme stress on a constant basis. There is one easy way to mitigate this risk. Every so often, everyone needs to just RELAX. **Mandatory time off, paid vacations, maternity leave & sick days all allow people to RESET.**

Once you achieve success most people decide to relax, for others this is quite difficult. Many people truly desire to continue working as long as they can & as hard as they can. This can be stressful on the body, no matter how much you enjoy work. We are not machines.

CHAPTER 10

SLOW & STEADY : 3 Ways to relax
- Meditate, Celebrate & Create

One thing machines do not do is relax. They keep working until they break. This is not a great strategy for farmers, employees, owners or investors in any business. There must be a balance to life or else we will simply run ourselves into the ground.

It is common for busy business owners to simply forget to relax. They don't prioritize it. In reality relaxing is incredibly important for your ability to work. You should prioritize it.
You need to determine when you are going to do so & commit, just like work.

I will be honest, I actually relaxed too much for a while & this led to very little getting done. At the time, I was actually ok with it, because I had a small goal of living offgrid on a farm.
I choose to relax now in the morning for a short period of time & at night before going to bed.

This slower pace of life should not be looked down upon. There is nothing wrong with a simple life that is humble & honest. Not everyone needs to have large goals. I have learned in life that just having a goal is enough to make most people happy.

Once most people complete their goal they feel perfectly comfortable relaxing. One should be so lucky to set a goal, reach it & relax having accomplished their desire. It is an endless jouney & constant struggle to continually change goals or pursue perfection.

Instead of perfection I offer you this alternative : Consider mak-

ing a plan, achieve it & relax. You can do this repeatedly for your whole life & achieve XXXLarge goals all along the way.
By prioritizing the celebration of success & achievement of goals, you can practice relaxing.

Each time you finish a week of work there is a time to reflect back on what you have achieved. I urge you to take the last day of the week & relax while reflecting on your successes. If you have not succeeded yet & are still struggling, you may not want to relax just yet.

The 3 ways I encourage successful/stressful people to relax are based on my own experiences. After traveling the world & starting many businesses I have found these to truly help.
They are based but I highly suggest that you use them regularly, making healthy habits.

1. Mediate - When your mind seems cluttered or overwhelmed, you may need to empty it
2. Celebrate - After a significant accomplishment you should commemorate it & relax
3. Create - In times of tension or slow period, creating art or music can be therapeutic

Meditation is often mistaken for hippy talk or guru nonsense, but science disagrees. After much research using brain scanning equipment to monitor activity in meditators, It has been proven that the mental exercise can reset the brain & allow the organs to relax.

This period of rest & lack of tension in the mind means that there is a chemical balance. Instead of flooding the receptors with reactions to stimulation, meditation provides harmony.
Without the stress of complex thought, constant emotions or conlic, the brain is able to heal.

Meditation can be achieved easily by finding a comfortable place to sit in a chair or the ground. I highly encourage people to sit directly on the earth beneath a tree to meditate.

This practice of sitting quietly can be extended for anywhere from 3 to 30 minutes or more.

Simply sit on the ground with your eyes closed, breathing slowly & think of nothing. Clearing your mind is difficult at first, but do not worry, try to let go by breathing out. Breathe in fresh air & each time you breath out slowly, exhale any negative thoughts.

I will not go into the complexities of mantras or the different breathing techniques. The point of encouraging you to meditate is for you to relax, do not overthink this process.

Meditation is what you make it. Many people pray in meditation. Some think of Science.

You can meditate on anything you want. I personally focus on manifesting my dreams. I focus my energy on visualizing what I want & the path required to get to that level. I will sit in silence thinking about my dreams & I encourage you to do the same regularly.

Celebration is often mistaken for partying or being wild or getting hammered or wasted. Celebrating in excess & not knowing your limits with substances can be very harmful. When I talk about celebrating I mean having fun with others surrounding an occasion.

That occasion certainly does not need to include alcohol or cake or Coca Cola to be relaxing. A celebration between myself & my partner now often involves a nice piece of chocolate. Sitting together looking at our work on the farm, while eating chocolate is a celebration.

I also enjoy wine & would like to take this opportunity to address why wine is important. Wine is a wonderful thing in my opinion. There is of course a thing as too much wine. I highly discourage you from drinking too much wine while celebrating. I have done it.

I will tell you that there is nothing less relaxing than a hangover from too much wine. There is nothing classy about having too much wine & falling over on a regular basis. If you are not careful you will be labeled as a heavy drinker & destroy your reputation.

The nice thing about wine is you don't have to drink it fast or drink alot to enjoy it. It is very classy to have a glass of wine, enjoy your buzz, relax & not finish the bottle. Some people even meditate over a good glass of wine, sitting eyes closed appreciating it.

I personally enjoy plants more than I like wine. There are many plants that can help you relax. When I was very young I learned about herbal teas, burning herbs & smoking herbs.
Lavender & chamomile are my favorite plants for tea, I like sage for burning & lots of cannabis.

That's right I am a huge advocate of eating & smoking cannabis to relax. It is not for everyone. I feel that everyone has a choice how they relax, I personally like relaxing with a big spliff. Some people do not like THC & prefer CBD which is very relaxing & less expensive.

I have found that many people on the planet like these same plants, however some do not. To be honest the world is changing & I think the stigma around cannabis is relaxing. People have seen the medical research & data behind the effects it has on health.

Some people have even reported that it helps them be a better parent, boss or artist. I personally have found that Sativa plants make me more creative & social, so that's my jam.
I love tropical sativas & CBD mixed together in the morning & Indica at night to sleep.

Creation can be liberating, therapeutic & healing all at once.

When we create art we are free. Art can be made in the form of dancing, painting, drawing, sculpting, writing or anything.
You can create with your hands, your mind, your voice & your feet, whatever feels right.

I have created so many things in my life, that were not for profit, they were to relax. I spent a lot of my life just creating, because it helps me release my feelings in a positive way.
Dancing & music have helped me more through intense relationships than any therapist.

When we create with our feet & move our body we are expressing who we are. There was a time in my life when dancing was incredibly important & allowed me to grow.
I traveled the world seeking places to dance & people to dance with. Until I found one I loved.

One of the greatest things about creating the life you dream of is that inevitably you will find a partner who wants to join you. The greatest thing we can hope for in life is not success, it is companionship. I often write about business, but without my partner I wouldn't have one.

Companionship of course is not required in life, however I have done much study that indicates without a social life or partner, humans statistically live shorter lives. A companion could be a pet who you take care of or a friend you love deeply.

I write this at the end of the book to make sure I have given a fully balanced account of life. Life is not all about work or success or following the rules, you do not need to 3x everything!
Life is about balance. Life is about relaxing. Life is about loving. Life is about respecting.

You should strive to work hard & everyday be tired from doing what you love. You should not feel the need to overwork yourself or stress yourself out though. There is a happy balance in the middle that allows you time to relax & enjoy your life.

The goal is balance. You achieve it through hard work. The way to succeed is to relax routinely. There is a constant pressure to work when what we need is to be happy with our goals. If we have goals & we reach them, we should be able to relax & celebrate our work.

This balance in life is what I seek. I am not a guru or an expert. I am just a man. I have observed different cultures & what I have seen is amazing. So many amazing men & women living, working & creating things together.

My hope is that as you finish this book you start to realize how lucky you are. You always have 3 options & now you can relax having finished your goal. If you have a goal of reading a book every week you will be smarter by the end of the year.

I wanted to end this book by saying how much of a pleasure it has been to write for you. I wrote this inspired by the different experiences of my life & to express how you can think differently if you are stuck. I know that there will be times when everything seems overwhelming, remember to relax.

Let this book be a reminder that you can do whatever you put your mind to. You may need to revisit this book if you feel down or lend it to someone who needs a boost. Books are incredible because you can pass information & share experiences with friends.

If you have ever wanted to write a book I encourage you to do so. It is a wonderful exercise. I think you will be great at whatever you decide to do next. My grandma Mary always said :
" Just do your best." That is all we can do sometimes, tomorrow will be a new day.

- The End -

WRITTEN BY SIMON HAWK

Afterthought

How To Fall Asleep *Faster*

If you happen to have read this book late at night & it did not make you fall asleep, rather you are wide awake thinking about how to 3x your profits. Don't worry it's going to happen.
It is incredibly important for business owners & entrepreneurs to get adequate sleep.

While everyone needs a different amount of sleep, most people function best on 6-9 hours of sleep. I have found that my partner who is a female, sleeps more than I, she also falls asleep alot faster than I. This got me thinking about ways to fall asleep faster.

So I started researching.

I read a lot of white papers, I poured over books, I analyzed research, I read hundreds of different perspectives & articles on what influences our sleep patterns.

I figured if I could determine 3 ways to help people fall asleep faster, it might help.

So after all of my reading & research I have concluded that there really is a top 3.

Aside from people with serious sleeping disorders or chemical imbalances or bad beds,

There are 3 strategies that stood out to me as seriously effective solutions for falling asleep.

1. Books - I didn't design this book to be boring & put you to sleep, if it did, you are welcome.

2. Lights - Any LED light, especially a phone will keep you up. Turn them off & dim the lights.

3. Herbs - Many herbs can help you sleep, try Cannabis, CBD, Lavender, Hops or Melatonin.

These 3 short term strategies can help most people to overcome sleeping issues.

To be honest most people just need to turn off the tv, turn off the phone & turn off the lights. If you are freaking out about drama, stress or problems, you need to relax & disconnect.

Take the weight of the world off & let go of the past memories or problems of the day. Each night we must forgive those who have wronged us & release any guilt or shame. The mind is a powerful thing & the pressure to succeed or expand can be overwhelming.

It is best to realize that we often put all of this pressure on ourselves. This is mental weight. Constantly lighting physical weights will leave you stronger, but mental weight wears on one. The weight of success is a heavy burden & we should only desire what we can carry.

When we speak about sleeping faster, it should be mentioned that exercise does help immensely to get rid of extra energy that could be keeping you up at night.

The combination of a healthy diet & regular exercise can greatly improve your schedule.

Avoiding caffeine & sugary foods or beverages after 8pm is important to sleeping easily.
A diet that is diverse with organic fruits & vegetables can contribute to a healthier system.

Reducing your intake late at night can help to let the body rest fully instead of digesting.

Hopefully this information is incredibly boring & if you are trying to fall asleep it's working.

Soothing sounds such as classical music, running water or forest sounds help some people.

If all else fails, there is always love. Remember to love yourself people. Loving yourself is good.

Remember to love your partner. Share & communicate directly about why you can't sleep. Many times partners are blissfully unaware that we suffer while they sleep.

It is important to ask for help or get assistance if you have serious sleep problems. There is no shame in asking for help. I hope that this book sheds some light on things. I wrote it to help you look at life in a positive light. There is so much to love about life.

I want you to be in love with your life, because that is what you have, a beautiful life.

What you do with your life is your choice, I encourage you to do beautiful things with it.

Help people. Teach people. Start businesses. Create Art. Sell Products & Be Successful!

I really do believe you are capable of whatever you put your mind to do.

All that I ask is that you do your best & pay it forward. You can always give someone a book.

If you know someone who needs to read this, give them this book or send a copy.

There is nothing like sharing knowledge, especially if it helps you grow or fall asleep :)

Dulce Suenos

www.ingramcontent.com/pod-product-compliance
Lightning Source LLC
Chambersburg PA
CBHW070801050426
42452CB00012B/2435